My very first experience with a cigar was, in a word, unlucky. It was an especially cold winter during high school, and an ice storm had just hit and closed school. My parents were away on vacation, which allowed me quiet time around the house. The first thing I did was go down to the most fascinating room of the house—my father's office in the basement where he smoked his pipes and enjoyed his cigars. I can recall the rich, sweet aroma of tobaccos that permeated the leather of his chair. The smell was like a friendly ghost that invisibly lingered about his male sanctuary. The walls were lined with his vast pipe collection, and gorgeous, dark brown cigars filled his humidors. I found his smoking robe and put it on, popped in the movie *Amadeus* and settled into his chair. I was feeling quite regal. I glanced over at his mahogany humidor and liquor cabinet. Like Odysseus' sirens, they called to me. My dad always made a drink when he enjoyed his smokes, so I poured a little whiskey and water into a glass, and selected what would be my first cigar. I did a somewhat sloppy job of cutting and lighting it, but the draw and the aroma were decadent. I leaned back in my father's chair and soaked it all in. Like a king.

I did not yet understand the finesse of smoking a cigar and rushed through it, puffing frequently and feverishly. Not long after, the feeling of regality turned into extreme nausea, as I rushed out the door into the snowy back yard! But despite this memorable initiation, my great passion for cigars and the cigar life had begun.

Fast-forward twenty years. As president of CAO, we are always finding better ways to produce the very best cigars in the world. One thing that attracts me to the cigar lifestyle is that cigars create a bonding experience, a bridge between people. Whether it is to escape life's pressures, celebrate, or relax, cigar smoking brings friends and strangers together. Few things in life unite people in the same way.

I was recently the guest-of-honor at an event where CAO gifted cigars to more than four hundred United States Marines stationed at Quantico in Virginia. During the evening, their general—a man who had led more than ten thousand troops in Iraq—approached me and introduced himself. We discussed our mutual passion—cigars—for hours, as though we were long lost comrades. While this military giant and I probably have very little in common, a cigar brought us together. This, my friends, is one of life's great joys and what the cigar life is all about.

Tim Ozgener
CAO President

To John Konig for having introduced me to the 'feeling of well-being'
imparted by a good cigar. And Edward Sahakian for being
the world's best cigar merchant.

© 2008 Assouline Publishing
601 West 26th Street, 18th floor
New York, NY 10001, USA
Tel.: 212 989-6810   Fax: 212 647-0005
www.assouline.com

Color separation by Luc Alexis Chasleries

ISBN: 978 2 75940 268 7
Printed in China

CIGAR STYLE

NICK FOULKES

ASSOULINE

❝ He sat down, tucked the tiger-skin robe around his legs and lit a cigar. 'How is it you don't smoke? A cigar is not just a pleasure—it's the crown and hallmark of pleasure. Ah, this is life!' **❞**

Leo Tolstoy, *Anna Karenina*

many people have written many things about cigars, but by putting these words into the mouth of his sybaritic creation Prince Stepan Arkadyich Oblonsky, Tolstoy sums up—probably better than anyone else—the mysterious allure that a tube of matured tobacco leaves has exerted and continues to exert over a sizable proportion of the world's population.

Even today, as many countries gradually restrict the use of tobacco, the cigar continues to enjoy a totemic status. In film, literature, and art, the cigar still has its place as a signifier of the good life and a symbol of hope and celebration. A cigar is special, far more than a vehicle for nicotine ingestion into the bloodstream. For that mere purpose there are cigarettes and chewing tobacco. Today, smoking a cigar is a symbolic and defiant act of pure pleasure.

To ignite a cigar—to watch the glossy tobacco transmute into silvery ash and blue smoke and to savor its complex and lingering flavors—is to practice a ritual that has been performed for centuries by kings and courtesans, prime ministers and presidents, authors and artists. It is a ritual that has its roots in the sacred and mystical practices of the pre-Columbian Americas, in a time long before Cristóbal Colón—or Christopher Columbus, as he is more commonly known—and Amerigo Vespucci, before Hernán Cortés and Juan Ponce de León "discovered" what they arrogantly called the New World.

"It all started in the New World," wrote Guillermo Cabrera Infante in his 1985 book *Holy Smoke*, "where smoking was not for gentlemen but for sorcerers—and for the incumbent Indian chief, who wore the feathers." The Taíno tribe cultivated tobacco for religious purposes and consumed quantities large enough to bring about a trancelike state that opened their minds to moments of epiphany and the elucidation of eternal truths. Perhaps it was because they were in such a euphoric state that the conquistadores had no trouble subduing the indigenous peoples and taking their riches and their love of tobacco back to the Old World.

t hus began what Infante romantically calls "the five-century-old relationship between the European gentleman and his smoke." Even though the gentlemen of Europe did not consume the amount of tobacco necessary to induce visions and hallucinations, the cigar has long been associated with creativity and seen as a stimulus to intellectual activity. Victor Hugo put it rather well when he said that "tobacco is the plant that converts thoughts into dreams." It was through a haze of the blue-gray smoke of his cigar that Sigmund Freud peered into the secret world of men's and women's dreams. The cigar imposes leisure on the smoker and gives him time to think, as P. J. O'Rourke put it in a 1998 interview with *Cigar Aficionado* magazine: "I really think cigar smoking does make you smarter. Or maybe it just makes you sit still long enough to be smart."

however, for almost as long as there have been devotees of what Iain Gately calls *la diva nicotina* in his book of the same title, there have been others who are implacably opposed to her. A time-honored, tobacco-related ritual has been the intervention of the state in the private pleasure of extracting comfort and solace from smoking. One would have thought that the king of England would have more pressing matters on his mind, but in 1604, James I published his polemic pamphlet *A Counterblaste to Tobacco*. In the course of this colorful rant, he touches upon themes that are as familiar today as they were more than four centuries ago: the effects of peer pressure, the health risks, and the alleged antisocial nature of *Nicotiana tabacum*. The way His Majesty saw it, smoking was "a custom loathsome to the eye, hateful to the Nose, harmful to the brain, dangerous to the Lungs, and in the black, stinking fume thereof, nearest resembling the horrible Stygian smoke of the pit that is bottomless." And yet for all of his rhetorical vigor and concern for his subjects' well-being, James I did not outlaw tobacco, he merely taxed it. This hypocritical custom is still practiced by governments throughout the world today. In spite of it, tobacco and tobacco culture have flourished. The drug of choice of the indigenous shaman became an essential accessory of the gentleman.

t he cigar was largely a quirk of the Hispanic world; however, Napoleon changed all that when he added Spain to his European empire. Operating on the principle that her enemy's enemy was her friend, France's natural foe, Britain, sided with the Spanish guerrillas and an up-and-coming young English military commander, Sir Arthur Wellesley. Together, they did such a good job of clearing the French out of Spain that when Wellesley came back to England, he was made the Duke of Wellington. Among the souvenirs that the returning veterans of the Peninsular War brought with them were curious little tubes of tobacco. By the time Wellington was called to serve his country in the battle that became known as Waterloo, the cigar was already part of the kit of the well-prepared British officer. The cigar even made the torrential downpour on the night before the battle bearable. "Dear weed! What comfort, what consolation dost thou not impart to the wretched," rhapsodised artillery officer Alexander Cavalié Mercer in his book *Journal of the Waterloo Campaign*. "With thee a hovel becomes a palace. What stock of patience is there not enveloped in one of thy brown leaves!"

The British gentleman had discovered that he enjoyed cigars, and as Britain became the dominant military, political, and cultural power of the nineteenth century, so the cigar became a part of the aristocratic mien of the gentleman, as much a part of the "done thing" as dressing for dinner and cultivating a stiff upper lip (the latter a useful attribute for keeping a cigar in one's mouth). Even though Queen Victoria hated cigars, her male subjects, including her eldest son, adored them.

It is surely no coincidence that my favorite works of art and fiction from this period involve cigars. In William Powell Frith's most famous panoramic, narrative canvas, *The Derby Day* (1858), a young, elegant man lounges against a barouche, hands in his pockets, watch chain and seals hanging from his waistcoat, and a cigar dangling nonchalantly from the corner of his mouth. If Frith was the master of the panoramic in painting, then William Makepeace Thackeray was his equal in words. And just as Frith gave us the young blade leaning against a carriage full of ladies, Thackeray created *Vanity Fair*'s Rawdon Crawley, the mustache-twirling Flashman-like officer of dragoons whose fortunes fluctuated with his luck at the gaming tables. It is over a cigar that the book's antiheroine, the coquettish Becky Sharp, steals his heart.

> "You don't mind my cigar, do you, Miss Sharp?" says the Captain. Miss Sharp loved the smell of a cigar outdoors beyond everything in the world and tastes one in the prettiest way possible. She gave it a little puff, a little scream, and a little giggle and all of this restored the delicacy to the Captain, who twirled his moustache, and straightway puffed it into a blaze that glowed quite red in the dark plantation, and swore—"Jove—aw—Gad—aw—it's

the finest segaw I ever smoked in the world aw," for his intellect and conversation were alike brilliant and becoming to a heavy young dragoon.

a postmodern deconstruction of Thackeray's novels, in which characters smoke cigars at all possible times—whether they are happy or sad, solitary or in the company of others, walking or in carriages, outside or indoors—doubtless gives phallocentric critics much to think about. However, before they get too carried away, Freud has a word of warning: "Sometimes a cigar is just a cigar." Not, of course, that Britain's great poet of empire, Rudyard Kipling, agreed with the Viennese doctor. For Kipling, "a woman is only a woman, but a good cigar is a smoke." This, oft-quoted piece of cigar lore is part of his poem *The Betrothed*, in which a man has to choose between his fiancée, Maggie, and his cigars.

> We quarrelled about Havanas—we fought o'er a good cheroot.
> And I know she is exacting, and she says I am a brute.
> However, there is never really any doubt as to the decision that will be made.
> Which is the better portion—bondage bought with a ring,
> Or a harem of dusky beauties, fifty tied in a string?

Anyone who has ever seen a bundle of fifty "cabinet selection" cigars, the outer, or wrapper, leaves of each one suffused with what is almost a golden glow, will know how tempting they look, and by the poem's final couplet, the seductive cigars have triumphed and the engagement is at an end.

> Light me another Cuba—I hold to my first-sworn vows.
> If Maggie will have no rival, I'll have no Maggie for Spouse!

Kipling wrote this poem in 1890, a time when the cult of the cigar was probably at its strongest. Cigarettes, introduced to Western Europe after the Crimean War, were still considered a fashion item, smoked for effect by outré figures such as Oscar Wilde and by "emancipated" women. In contrast, the cigar spoke of the "manly" virtues of prosperity and solidity. A cigar was as much a part of correct attire for a gentleman as was, say, a top hat or a frock coat. As such, cigars cropped up in portraits of notable figures of the day, whether they were depicted by John Singer Sargent or Henri de Toulouse-Lautrec. And when the splendor of the Gilded Age in New York was evoked on film in Martin Scorsese's 1993 adaptation of Edith Wharton's *The Age of Innocence*, the ritual surrounding the clipping and smoking cigars was lovingly recreated.

However, this was America, and the cigars smoked by Newland Archer and his cronies in their smart evening clothes were only part of the story. Beyond the clubby surroundings of huge New York City mansions, in which titans of industry and finance plotted the future of the world in a haze of blue smoke, the country that was to become the world's most powerful was still being shaped by rough men doing rough jobs who smoked rough cigars. The Wild West, as portrayed in the famous spaghetti Westerns of the 1960s and 1970s, was a place where real men seldom shaved and rarely washed but almost always had thin black cheroots on the go.

this more rambunctious appreciation of the cigar was typified by the quondam steamboat pilot and failed miner-turned-journalist and author Samuel Clemens, better known as Mark Twain. Like most cigar-loving men of letters, Clemens came up with a good crop of aphorisms on the subject, the most famous of which concerned his unwillingness to go to heaven if smoking was not allowed. His appetite for cigars was heroic, and he favored quantity over quality; for instance, while writing the semi-autobiographical travel book *Roughing It*, he consumed ten cigars a day, and he made light of his consumption. As recounted in *The Wit and Wisdom of Mark Twain*, "I have made it a rule never to smoke more than one cigar at a time," he quipped. Another of his rules was "never to smoke when asleep and never to refrain when awake."

Besides, you could never tell when a cigar was going to come in handy. That same collection includes another telling anecdote: At a dinner in 1900, Twain, one of the great cigar smokers of the nineteenth century, met a young Winston Churchill, destined to become one the greatest cigar smokers of the twentieth. The two men stepped out for a cigar, and one guest remarked that whichever of the two, both fond of their own voices, "got the floor first would keep it." After a while, the two men returned, and Churchill said how much he had enjoyed their chat. When asked if he had enjoyed himself, "Mark Twain paused, puffed his cigar and said, 'I have had a good smoke.'"

i ndeed, for many years, "a good smoke" was a much cherished tenet of American democracy. From the occupation of the third president of the United States, a tobacco farmer named Thomas Jefferson, through the twenty-a-day cigar habit of the eighteenth, Ulysses Grant, to the somewhat less polite cigar-related tastes of the forty-second, Bill Clinton, tobacco has been associated with the presidency far longer than either the White House or its famed Oval Office. At the turn of the nineteenth and twentieth centuries, cigar politics loomed large in America: Since 1606, when the Spanish crown had sanctioned the commercial cultivation of tobacco in Cuba and other of its colonies, including Puerto Rico, Santo Domingo, and Venezuela, the fortunes of Latin America had become closely linked to the cigar. According to Andrew and Nathaniel Lande's illustrated history *The Cigar Connoisseur*, there was even a cigar brand called the Monroe Doctrine—its box sported an American clad in a star-spangled blue tailcoat, striped trousers, and a top hat, his arms around a couple of stereotypical Latin Americans, one dressed as a matador, the other in a sombrero.
And when America, in particular future president Theodore Roosevelt, intervened in the domestic squabble between Spain and its colony Cuba, cigars became even more of a part of American life. It took a superpower standoff, the

Cuban Missile Crisis, to get America to kick its Cuban cigar habit, and even then President John F. Kennedy could not bring himself to announce his trade embargo until his press secretary, Pierre Salinger, had laid his hands on one thousand of the president's favorite cigars, the Petit Upmann.

S till today, in spite of the best efforts of several administrations to demonize it, Cuba holds a particular allure for Americans, perhaps because the forbidden fruit is supposed to be sweeter, perhaps because the cigars are so wonderful, or perhaps because in the first half of the twentieth century Cuba was regarded more or less as a de facto state in the union. Cigar lover and American George Hamilton told me how, as a young man, he used to fly to Havana for dinner and dancing and be back in Palm Beach for breakfast, doubtless having enjoyed a cigar or two.

While Cuban cigars were smoked by wealthy connoisseurs, the quality of the basic cigars enjoyed by average Americans had been steadily improving since the 1870s, when many émigrés from Cuba, then still a Spanish colony, had settled in Florida, making Tampa a huge cigar-producing center. The state of the "five-cent cigar" was a barometer of the nation's relative prosperity. And by the beginning of the twentieth century, it was really not at all bad. Its ubiquity led to a blue-collar cigar culture unlike anything in the Old World.

I remember once being driven past Yankee Stadium in a taxi by a driver who fondly reminisced about how, as a young man, he had gone to the stadium and how every man at the ball game was smoking a cigar. The five-cent cigar was the cigar of the America depicted by Norman Rockwell and Edward Hopper, and it became a political rallying cry when Vice President Thomas Riley Marshall quipped that what America needed was a "really good five-cent cigar." His was a serious point about the economic woes of America after World War I, when rising prices had led to the disappearance of the five-cent cigar and when even the cigars sold for seven or eight cents were not that good. Cowboy-actor Will Rogers shot back with the razor-sharp riposte, "Our country has plenty of five-cent cigars, but the trouble is they charge fifteen cents for them."

first, the nickel cigar had tarnished the exclusive image of the cigar. Then, the nickel cigar priced itself out of the market. And finally, the stock market crash of 1929 meant that even if you found a smokable five-cent cigar, there was precious little to celebrate with it anyway. Once again, the cigar's fortunes were linked to a war. Across the Atlantic, Mark Twain's garrulous dinner companion finally became prime minister of the United Kingdom, and Sam Clemens would have been proud of how Winnie puffed his way to victory. In Churchill's meaty hand, a cigar meant defiance; it meant freedom; it meant victory. On one of my visits to Cuba, I met an old man who claimed to have rolled some cigars for Churchill when the British statesman toured the Rome y Julieta factory. It was after this visit that the Clemenceau size (named for Georges Clemenceau, yet another wartime leader) was renamed Churchill.

Given that he was such an admirer of Churchill's, it is odd that Ian Fleming did not make James Bond a cigar smoker. Instead, the 007 of the novels favored Morlands cigarettes. It was left to the on-screen interpreters of the role to introduce the world's most famous secret agent to the joys of the cigar: Roger Moore first made Bond a cigar smoker, a habit that was continued by Pierce Brosnan, who revived the franchise during the 1990s. In fact, part of the 2002 Bond film *Die Another Day* was set in a cigar factory in Havana.

Ironically, the same scene could take place today on American soil, where homegrown cigar makers such as CAO have become renowned for excellence.

•

It is somewhat ironic that recent years have seen a comeback for the cigar, just as health warnings and smoking restrictions have been stepped up. Anyone choosing to smoke cigars today requires plenty of those Churchillian virtues of pluck, defiance, and determination. As the U.S. surgeon general continues to warn darkly of the consequences of smoking and as the enjoyment of cigars is curtailed in such cities as New York, popular culture continues to celebrate and flaunt the cigar with an almost perverse glee. If anything, as enjoying cigars becomes more difficult in real life, their use in cinema becomes more extravagant. Perhaps the clearest alignment of cigar smoking with such virtues as bravery and patriotism and a gung-ho, never-say-die optimism comes in the 1996 film *Independence Day*. How does all-American heartthrob Will Smith celebrate after a busy day spent learning to fly a spaceship, piloting it into the heart of an extraterrestrial military buildup, blowing up the invading force, and thus saving America (and by extension the rest of the world) from alien domination? By lighting up a cigar, of course.

In fact, it wouldn't surprise me if Will Smith had been reading a bit of Evelyn Waugh. As this most English of novelists was fond of saying: "The most futile and disastrous day seems well spent when it is reviewed through the blue, fragrant smoke of a Havana cigar."

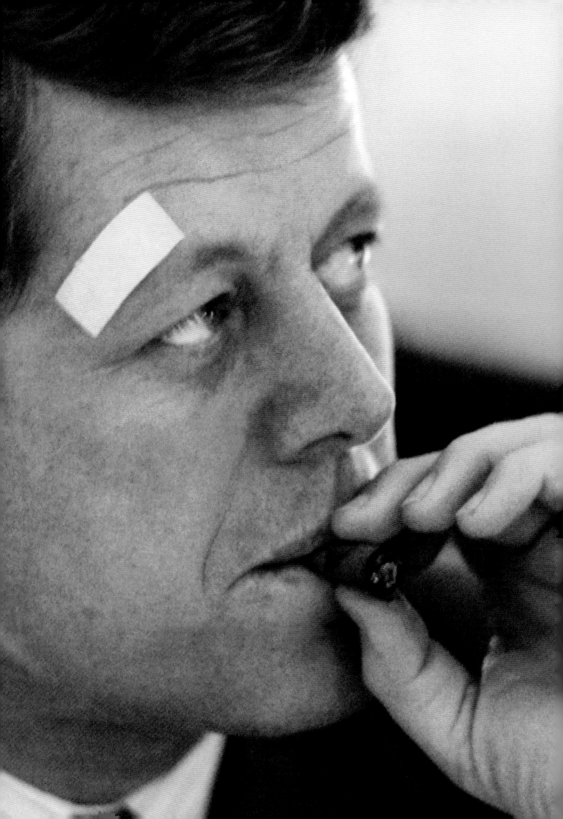

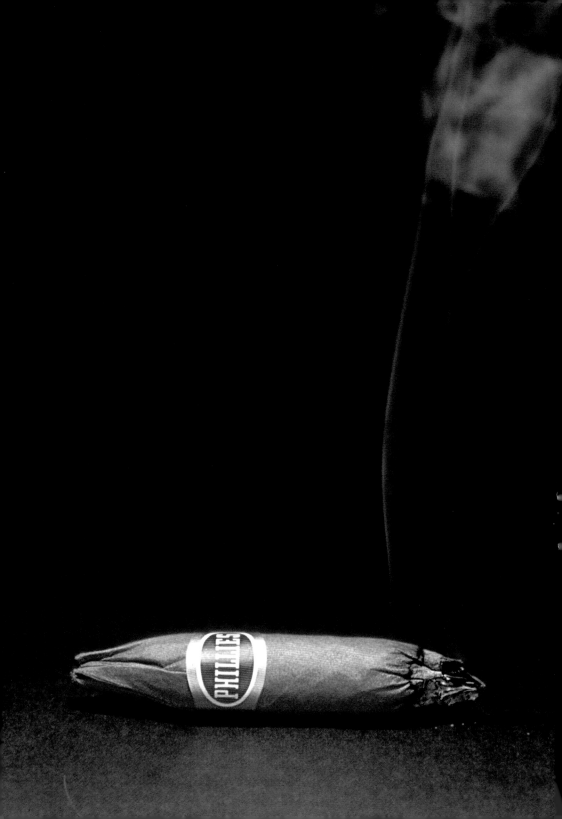

" Gentlemen, you may smoke. "

Winston Churchill

Joseph H. Sulkowski

" Tobacco is the plant that
converts thoughts into dreams. "

Victor Hugo

SMOKER

LOS REYES
DE ESPAÑA.

REGIAS

Chronology

900 AD: A ceramic vessel dated back to the 10th century is discovered in a Mayan site in Uaxactun, Guatemala. The vessel portrays a man smoking what appears to be a type of cigar.

1603: Cuban government decrees that the sale of tobacco to foreigners is punishable by death.

1604: King James I of England releases an analysis of the ill effects of cigar smoking, titled *The Counterblaste to Tobacco*.

1612: The first United States tobacco plantation is set up in Virginia.

1700s: Variations of "cigar"—seegar and segar—appear in the dictionary.

1715: The Spanish government sets up a monopoly on the tobacco trade and sells tobacco at fixed prices abroad.

1762: The cigar arrives in the United States when the Revolutionary War general, Israel Putnam returns from Cuba with Havanas and tobacco.

1790: Cigar manufacturing spreads to France and Germany.

1810: The sophisticated branding of cigars begins in Cuba. The first two brands are B. Rencurrel and Hija de Cabanas y Carbajal.

1812: The social phenomenon of cigar smoking takes off in France and Britain, when troops return with the smoking habit they adopted from the Spanish.

1817: King Ferdinand VII puts an end to the monopoly of the tobacco trade in Cuba, allowing cigar production and sales to begin.

1837: Ramon Allones uses lithography on the exterior of the cigar box.

1962: Pierre Salinger, Kennedy's press secretary, reports that President John F. Kennedy ordered one thousand Cuban 1200 H. Upmann Petit Corona Cigars and Philippine Alhambras. The next day, February 7th, Kennedy imposes a trade embargo on Cuba.

1993: Martin Scorsese's 1993 adaptation of Edith Wharton's *The Age of Innocence* premieres, recreating the tradition of careful clipping and smoking of cigars.

2005: Premium cigar manufacturer CAO International, Inc. debuts the CAO The Sopranos Edition, a special cigar line to commemorate the award-winning television series.

A **cigar** burning in an ashtray. © JUPITERIMAGES/Agence Images/Alamy.

Cigar Style

Cuban Havana Cohiba Behike cigars, considered the world's most expensive cigars at $440 each. © Susana Vera/Reuters/CORBIS.
George Harrison and Ringo Starr smoking cigars in London at the Carl Allen Awards, March 23, 1964. © Getty Images.

A cigar-smoking Winston Churchill, photographed in Canada, 1929. © Bettmann/CORBIS.
The rising curls of smoke from a cigar. © Chloe Johnson/Alamy.

Tobacco plantation worker "Ranchero," Nicaragua. Courtesy of John Chiasson.
A wrapped bundle of hand-rolled cigars, Dominican Republic. © Wayne Eastep/Getty Images.

A cigar and ashtray on a leather armchair. © Christian Schmidt/zefa/CORBIS.
Chess players at the Spanish Club at the Teatro Garcia Lorca in Havana, Cuba. © Rene Burri/Magnum Photos.

President John F. Kennedy smoking a cigar during a White House conference. © Paul Schutzer/Time & Life Pictures/Getty Images.
Jacqueline Kennedy Onassis and Aristotle Onassis relax during a tour of Egypt in 1974. © Bettmann/CORBIS.

Workers in a tobacco growing field, Nicaragua. Courtesy of CAO International.
Tobacco hanging in the CAO Fábrica de Tabacos curing barn, Nicaragua. Courtesy of CAO International.

A neat stack of carefully rolled tobacco leaves. © Patrick Jantet.
A man smoking a cigar in Havana. © Patrick Jantet.

Brigitte Bardot smoking a slim cigar in 1971. © Terry O'Neill/Getty Images.
Actor Groucho Marx smoking a cigar in 1952. © Philippe Halsman/
Magnum Photos.

Pablo Picasso in his studio in Paris, circa 1920–1930. © Bettmann/CORBIS.
Cigar with ash in black and white. © Joe Mikos/Getty Images.

Handmade cigars at a factory in Cuba. © Per Eriksson/Getty Images.
Inspecting the leaf, at the CAO Fábrica de Tabacos in Nicaragua. Courtesy
of John Chiasson.

An artisan expertly rolls the tobacco leaves. © Patrick Jantet.
A wooden tobacco press used primarily for hand-rolled cigars. © Patrick Jantet.

The famous gangster Al Capone smoking a cigar on his way to an Atlanta
penitentiary, 1932. © Bettmann/CORBIS.
Profile of Cuban revolutionary Ernesto "Che" Guevara smoking a cigar in 1964.
© Bob Parent/Hulton Archive/Getty Images.

A smoking Phillies Blunt. Anthony Verde/Time Life Pictures/Getty Images.
World's Greatest Flyer, 5 Cent Cigar Cigar Box Label, © 1927–1939, © Swim
Ink 2, LLC/CORBIS; *Morro Castle, Tobacos Superiores Esquisitos, El Trabajo, Spana
Cuba* and *Fabricantes de Cigaros*, © Paris Pierce/Alamy; *Aristada* Cigar Label,
1890–1930 and *Snap Shot* Cigar Label 1925, © Blue Lantern Studio/CORBIS.

Actress Faye Dunaway in the role of Bonnie Parker from Arthur Penn's film, *Bonnie and Clyde*, in 1966. © Hulton Archive/Getty Images.
Woman smoking a cigar. © mediacolor's/Alamy.

Bundle of cigars in black and white. © Hitoshi Nishimura/Getty Images.
Supplier of famous Partagas Cuban cigars, Cuba. © Bill Bachmann/Alamy.

A selection of CAO Cigars in wooden molds. Photo Credit: Courtesy of CAO International.
Orson Welles smoking a cigar in the filming of *Chimes at Midnight*, 1964. © Nikolas Tikhomiroff/Magnum Photos.

A collage of various cigar labels. © Patrick Jantet.
Some of the most refined palates belong to women. © Patrick Jantet.

Tim Ozgener, President of CAO. Courtesy of John Chiasson.

Women and men in the factory rolling tobacco leaves that will soon hug the body of Havana cigars. © Patrick Jantet.

Cigar Aficionado, original oil on canvas by Joseph H. Sulkowski. Permission to reprint by the artist.

Employees stand on the balcony of the Partagas Fábrica de Tabacos in Havana, Cuba, at the 150th Anniversary of the company, September 15, 1995. © Stephen Ferry/Liaison/Getty Images.

CAO Founder Cano A. Ozgener and his beloved dog, TonTon. Courtesy of John Chaisson.

Various sizes of CAO Brazilia Cigars. Courtesy of CAO International.
A silver hand holding a smoking cigar. © Sagel & Kranefeit/zefa/CORBIS.

British filmmaker Alfred Hitchcock during the filming of *The Birds*, 1962.

French actor and singer/songwriter Jacques Dutronc in 1980. © Tony Frank/ Sygma/CORBIS.
CAO 65th Anniversary Moda Cigar. Courtesy of CAO International; CAO L'Anniversaire Cameroon Churchill Cigar. Courtesy of CAO International.

Smoker's Club print, 19th century. © Bettmann/CORBIS.

Los Reyes de Espana Coronas Regias Cigar Label. © Patrick Jantet.

Illustration of a man smoking a cigar. © Eddie Cathey/Illustration Works/ Getty Images.
Habanas Quality Cigars illustration. © Steve Forney.

Acknowledgments

The publisher would like to thank the following people for their contributions to the book: Katie Sulkowski of Literary Trust, Inc.; Tim Ozgener, Cano Ozgener, Mike Conder and Jon Huber of CAO International; Dilcia Johnson at Corbis; Larry Van Cassele at Getty Images; Michael Shulman of Magnum Photos; Koshy Oommen and Pramod Raveendran of ALAMY; Joseph H. Sulkwoski; John Chaisson; Patrick Jantet; Steve Forney; and Luc Alexis Chasleries.